COVENANT • BIBLE • STUDIES

The Lord's Prayer

Mary Sue H. Rosenberger

faithQuest ◆ Brethren Press

Unless otherwise noted, scripture quotations are from the Revised Standard Version of the Bible, copyrighted 1946, 1952, 1971, 1973, 1977 by the National Council of Churches of Christ in the USA, Division of Education and Ministry.

Cover design by Jeane Healy

97 96 95 94 93   5 4 3 2

International Standard Book Number: 0-87178-541-2

Library of Congress Cataloging-in-Publication Data
Rosenberger, Mary Sue H.
    The Lord's Prayer
        p. cm. — (Covenant Bible study series)
    1. Bible. N.T. Lord's Prayer—Textbooks. I. Title. II. Series
BT381.2.B65 1989   223'.206
ISBN 0-87178-541-2

Manufactured in the United States of America

Contents

Foreword

Two of the earliest prayers I remember began like this: "God is great and God is good, and we thank him for our food ..." and "Now I lay me down to sleep ..." Perhaps you, too, remember these or similar prayers from early childhood. Such memorized prayers were soon followed by the simple spoken prayers of "Thank you, God, for ..."

These early childhood prayers were just the beginning. Prayer continues into adulthood. We need and want to grow in our understanding of prayer and our prayer life. We turn to the scriptures to see how the people of God of old talked with and listened to God. We learn about prayer from the lives of the saints, and from people of faith today.

Our best guide for prayer, however, is still that given by Jesus, known to us as the Lord's Prayer. Learned first perhaps in Sunday school or in our parents' home, this prayer "grows" with us through the years. Words first memorized become a vital and living spiritual resource for adult life.

This Bible study on the Lord's Prayer will help your group study this special prayer phrase by phrase, looking also at other biblical texts which illustrate the concepts found in the prayer. One of the goals of the study is that you may discover in this prayer ways to deal faithfully with the joys and stresses of life today.

Welcome to this study of the Lord's Prayer, a relational Bible study designed for small group settings within the congregation. As your group begins in this study, you will want to keep in mind some important features of relational Bible study:

1. The words of scripture relate to our lives and become alive for us today;
2. Each person contributes to the study ... each one shares the meaning that they find and helps bring meaning to others;
3. All persons are learners and all are leaders ... we all come needing to learn; we help lead each other to new discoveries.
4. Trust and vulnerability are needed ... we are vulnerable as we share out of life's experience, in relational Bible study, we learn to trust others and to be trustworthy;
5. Together a small group of learners gathers around the Word and discerns God's word for them today.

Relational Bible study has a strong biblical foundation. It is anchored in the covenantal history of God's people. We believe that God's empowerment comes to the community as its members gather to pray and to study, to share and to receive, to reflect and to act. The gathered community is necessary for growing in faith. Yet such growth does not just happen—it must be struggled for in the power of the Holy Spirit and in accord with the teachings of Jesus Christ.

Relational Bible study takes seriously the corporateness of our faith. The Body of Christ becomes a reality within the life of the group as each person contributes to their study, prayer, and work together. Each person's contribution is important as the group seeks the meaning of the text. "For just as the body is one and has many members, and all the members of the body, though many, are one body, so it is with Christ . . . Now you are the body of Christ and individually members of it" (1 Cor. 12:12,17).

Relational Bible study helps both persons and the group to claim the promise of the Spirit, to be open to the active working of ·the Holy Spirit in their midst. "For where two or three have met together in my name, I am there among them" (Matt. 18:20). "For God did not give us a spirit of timidity but a spirit of power and love and self-control" (2 Tim. 1:7).

Again, welcome to this relational Bible study of the Lord's Prayer. As you gather as a Sunday school class, a midweek Bible study group, in your church building, or in a member's home, may God's spirit richly guide and empower your study. May you dare to enter deeply into sharing with sisters and brothers. May you open yourselves to a new hearing of God's word for today.

May you approach this Bible study with the eagerness and the openness of the disciples as they asked, "Teach us to pray." May your prayer life be enriched, as your learn how to talk with and listen to God; and may the power of prayer be reflected in your daily walk.

June Adams Gibble
Elgin, Illinois

1

Prayer: An Act of Allegiance
Daniel 6; John 18:33-38

Preparation

1. Review a resource on prayer such as *Teach Me to Pray* by W. E. Sangster, printed by The Upper Room.

2. Recall to memory as many scriptural references to prayer as you can, especially the prayers of Jesus (Matt. 6:9-15, Mark 14:35-36, Luke 6:12-16; 23:34; 46; John 11:41-42; John 17; and others). Re-read as many as time allows.

Understanding

Introduction. After centuries of study, use, and abuse, is there anything new to be learned from the Lord's Prayer? Most of us learned it when we were children and use it in our private and personal times of prayer. It is prayed regularly in public worship and often in other public meetings. It is so familiar, in fact, that we run the risk of simply reciting it from habit rather than praying it from the heart with meaning.

Jesus never intended this prayer to become just a memory exercise or a religious formula to be recited in public meetings. In Matthew 6:9-13 he offers this prayer to his hearers as a contrast to those who prayed primarily for show. And Luke records in 11:2-4 that Jesus gave it to his disciples in response to their request. Having seen their Lord in prayer, they asked, "Lord, teach us to pray."

Most of us, when we are honest with ourselves, would like to make that same request of our Lord. Our study of Jesus' response to the request of his disciples will give opportunity for him to speak to us and remove that simple but profound prayer from rote memory to the depths of our hearts.

But to prepare ourselves properly for the study of the Lord's Prayer, we need first to become better acquainted with what prayer is. If it is not "so that everyone will see" (Matt. 6:5 TEV) nor "a lot of meaningless words (Matt. 6:7 TEV), what is it?

What is prayer? Webster defines prayer as an "act, practice or an instance of praying .... The offering of adoration, confession, supplication, thanksgiving to God or a god." James Montgomery's old hymn defines it differently:

> Prayer is the soul's sincere desire,
> Uttered or unexpressed,
> The motion of a hidden fire
> That trembles in the breast.
> Prayer is the burden of a sigh,
> The falling of a tear,
> The upward glancing of an eye,
> When none but God is near.
> Prayer is the simplest form of speech
> That infant lips can try;
> Prayer the sublimest strains that reach
> The Majesty on high.

Prayer, then, is communication with God. But our scripture texts for today's lesson would indicate that there is more to it than that.

An act of allegiance. In many public school classrooms, the school day begins with the students facing the American flag and reciting the pledge of allegiance to that flag. "I pledge allegiance to the flag," they begin, "and to the republic for which it stands."

Some years ago I became acquainted with a statement called "The Christian Pledge of Allegiance" which begins, "I pledge allegiance to Jesus Christ and to the Kingdom for which he died." Every Sunday or weekday when we attend worship and every time we pause in private or public prayer we are pledging allegiance to a power beyond the realities of the here and now. When we pray, we are declaring that we belong to God and to his kingdom. We are not totally subject to the petty pressures and politics of the present age.

Although it was a simple act of allegiance to God, kneeling in prayer got Daniel in serious trouble. But his lifelong relationship with his God was also what kept him safe through those times of trouble. Arthur Jeffrey says in his discussion of Daniel 6 in *The Interpreter's Bible*:

> The story indicates that religious faith is the bulwark against tyranny. It is important to note that the main issues of life do not change. The secondary circumstances are different, but the ultimate decisions each generation is called

upon to make are the same. Daniel had to face an edict of Darius that put the king above God. The author of the book was facing the threat of the Seleucids. We are always facing an arrogant nationalism that threatens to usurp the place of God . . . . The issues parade under different names, but they are still the same as Daniel faced.

What is the relationship of the church to the state? What is the relationship of the individual to his government? These are never easy questions to decide, and no final solution is ever found. Always there is an uneasy tension between church and state, with no clear dividing line. The one sure thing we know is that the state is not God, and man's allegiance is first of all to God.[1]

In John 18:33-38 we catch a vision of that kingdom to which we have first allegiance. It is a kingdom not defined nor bounded by this world. This kingdom is not founded on force but on free will and acts of personal commitment. It is a kingdom of truth-seekers who listen to Jesus as God's Truth-teller.

Church history. The Christian church has struggled throughout its history as to how to best express its allegiance to God's realm. Paul wrote to the Romans, "Do not be conformed to this world but be transformed by the renewing of your mind, that you may prove what is the will of God . . . " (12:2a). Matthew's record of Jesus' teachings on prayer cited above makes it clear that the early church desired to be more faithful to God than others had been.

From early on, Christians have sought to express their faithfulness to God's kingdom by nonconformity to their world in a variety of ways. Members of the Church of the Brethren, for example, have refused to take oaths as instructed in Matthew 5:33-37; they addressed each other only as Brother and Sister in faithfulness to Jesus' instructions in Matthew 23:8-9; they practiced the rite of feetwashing as part of their communion service in obedience to the Lord's example as recorded in John 13. Conforming to the instructions of their Lord was—and is—the way in which many Christians express their primary commitment to the kingdom of God.

Summary. In our world with its frantic pursuit of pleasure, power, and wealth, prayer is an act of allegiance to the kingdom of God. It witnesses to the reality and power of a kingdom "not of this world." It may direct towards nonconformity or even point towards a lion's den. But such an act of allegiance puts us in touch with that for which every human soul longs, a purpose for living. As Warren Groff says in his book *Prayer: God's Time and Ours!*:

To believe in God is to affirm that we have a nobler purpose for being than bone-grinding poverty, that we were not meant to grovel in bombed-out cities and defoliated countrysides, that we were not created for meaningless, routine jobs required to produce more and more things for a runaway economy, that we were not intended to endure lonely and isolated lives that follow from being forced to match the dehumanizing labels that box in the creative spirit.

Then where does prayer fit in? . . . It is a profoundly humanizing deed . . . [which] has its grounding in God's grace, but it is also our action. As such, it is a deeply personal expression.[2]

But, in the final analysis, the importance of prayer as an act of allegiance is not in the defining but in the doing. Montgomery's hymn continues:

O Thou, by whom we come to God,
The Life, the Truth, the Way,
The path of prayer Thyself hast trod;
Lord, teach us how to pray.

Discussion and Action

1. Do you agree that prayer is an act of allegiance? What does it say when we are "too busy to pray"?

2. Who—or what—are some of the modern-day tyrants that try to draw our allegiance away from God and his kingdom?

3. "Prayer changes things," a wall-hanging said. Is that true? If so, what does it change? Is the main value of prayer in the act or in the answer?

4. In preparation for next week, pray the Lord's Prayer daily in your own devotional time. Be prepared to jot down weekly a new insight you have learned from our study about this familiar prayer.

1. Arthur Jeffrey, *The Interpreter's Bible*, Vol. 6 (Nashville: Abingdon Press, 1956), p. 435.
2. Warren Groff, *Prayer: God's Time and Ours!* (Elgin, IL: Brethren Press, 1984), pp. 15-16.

2

Our Father . . .
Hosea 11:1-4; Luke 11:9-12

Preparation

1. Read the Lord's Prayer (Matt. 6:9-13 and Luke 11:2-4) from as many translations as possible. Read it in at least one foreign language if possible.

2. Memorize where it is found in the scriptures so that you will be able to find it easily during this study.

3. What are your earliest memories of the Lord's Prayer? From whom did you learn it? Where?

Understanding

Introduction. The simple, childlike phrase "Our Father . . . " introduces us to a devotional classic that has summoned the Christian world to its knees over the centuries. But not only is the Lord's Prayer a devotional masterpiece, it is a literary masterpiece as well.

It is brief and can be read or recited aloud in less than 30 seconds. It consists of only 57 words in the original Greek, 52 in the English translation. Three-fourths of the words used consist of only one syllable. It is simple but far from simplistic in what it shows us about the relationship God desires to have with us.

Relationships with God. In Luke's setting of the Lord's Prayer, which is probably the older of the two versions, the evangelist records that Jesus' disciples asked him to teach them to pray "as John taught his disciples." It was customary for a rabbi to teach his disciples a simple prayer which they might then regularly use. Jesus was following this pattern. William Barclay, in his commentary on this passage, says that this setting makes a difference in how we understand the prayer.

We must note, first of all, that this is a prayer which Jesus taught his *disciples* to pray . . . . The first thing to remember about the Lord's Prayer is that it is a prayer which only a disciple can pray; it is a prayer which only one who is pledged and committed to Jesus Christ can take upon his lips with any meaning. The Lord's Prayer is not a child's prayer, as it is so often regarded; it is, in fact, not meaningful for a child. The Lord's Prayer is not the Family Prayer as it is sometimes called, unless by the word *family* we mean *the family of the Church*. The Lord's Prayer is specifically and definitely stated to be the *disciple's* prayer; and only on the lips of a disciple has the prayer its full meaning. To put it in another way, the Lord's Prayer can only really be prayed when the man who prays it knows what he is saying, and he cannot know that until he has entered into discipleship.[1]

What kinds of relationships are implied in this "disciple's prayer" and in its introductory statement, "Our Father . . ." ? Perhaps a major part of the answer is in the fact that the pronouns used in this prayer are all plural—our, we, us. There is not an I, me, or mine in the entire prayer. It is clear that Jesus' intention was that the believer's relationship with God must be shared with others.

For most denominations, faith has always been a matter of sharing in community, never a private matter just between the believer and God. Baptism, love feast and communion, anointing for healing, the laying on of hands are all special experiences in which we mediate the grace of God to each other, sharing with the community of faith.

There is a profound truth in those two simple little words *Our Father*. God is my Father only as I acknowledge that he is also your Father and the Father of all who call upon the name of his son Jesus Christ.

Images of God. Clarence Jordan says in his book *Sermon on the Mount*:

> We have become accustomed to [using the word Father in addressing God] that we are not aware of the tremendous impact it must have had upon Jesus' original hearers. They were those who had been taught to stand in holy awe of the Most High. So greatly was he feared that they dared not even to use his name.[2]

The prevailing image of God in the Old Testament is of an awesome, powerful, and supremely holy Presence. Early in the history of the Israelite people, Moses had questioned the God who called him and asked his name. God replied, "I am who I am" (Exod. 3:14). The image of this unapproachable majesty continued as part of the Jewish consciousness.

There are, in the Old Testament, hints of a more loving image of the Almighty. The writer of Psalm 103 says, "As a father pities his children, so the Lord pities those who fear him" (v. 13). The prophet Isaiah, in telling of God's Messiah, says, "his name will be called 'Wonderful Counselor, Mighty God, Everlasting Father, Prince of Peace' " (9:6b).

But it was out of the anguish of his own symbolic and unhappy marriage to an unfaithful wife that the prophet Hosea gave us a new and more tender image of God. In Hosea 11:1-4 we read of God loving and calling to Israel as if to a child, teaching them to walk, taking up in healing arms, bending down and feeding them. These duties, traditionally performed by a mother, are descriptions of God's care of the chosen nation. Hosea saw God as tender, nurturing, and mother-like.

Jesus built upon a similar image in Luke 11:9-12 when he told a little story about gifts that loving fathers give to their sons. He went on to conclude in verse 13 (ENV), "If you then, who are evil, know how to give good gifts to your children, how much more will the heavenly Father give the Holy Spirit to those who ask him!" With the phrase "how much more," Jesus points us from that which we know—loving parents—to that which we know only dimly—the love of God.

Hymn writers and poets have used a variety of images in describing God. In our hymnals, we find God addressed as Star, Vine, Sculptor, Fire, and Guest. One contemporary poet described God in the act of creation as "like a mammy, bending over her baby."

Father, Mother, I AM, or Mammy—God transcends all images of which the human mind is capable. And when we lay aside the attempt to *see* God with our human minds, we will feel the arms of love surround us as we close our eyes and begin to pray, "Our Father . . . . "

Discussion and Action

1. Compare Matthew's and Luke's versions of the Lord's Prayer. Which do you prefer? Why?

2. Does God look—or act—like your father? your mother?

3. Does it make any difference to your faith that God is Heavenly Parent as well as Creator, Sustainer, etc.?

4. In an age of divorce and broken families, might another term communicate God better than Father?

5. In addition to those studied here, what other images of God are meaningful to you? from scripture? from other literature? from music? Share with the group as you are able.

6. Close your session by praying the Lord's Prayer together.

7. List something new you have learned today about the Lord's Prayer.

1. William Barclay, *The Daily Study Bible Series: The Gospel of Matthew,* Vol. 1 (Philadelphia: Westminster Press, 1958), p. 198.

2. Clarence Jordan, *Sermon on the Mount,* (Valley Forge: Judson Press, 1952), pp. 84-85.

God must be shared

3

Tell me something you remember from last week

... *Who Art in Heaven*
Daniel 2; Revelation 4

Preparation

1. Draw a picture of or describe in words your view of heaven. Where has it come from? From scripture? From other literature? From music?

2. As you study the suggested scripture texts for this session, also read through the hymn "Holy, Holy, Holy." Sing it over to yourself several times during the week. *Hymbee*

3. Read through or sing some other songs which speak of heaven, such as "Swing Low, Sweet Chariot," "I Got Shoes," "I See a New World Coming," "Let All Mortal Flesh Keep Silence," "Love Divine, All Loves Excelling," "O Joyous Easter Morning," "Be Thou My Vision," "Lo, a Gleam from Yonder Heaven," "O Jesus, Crucified for Me."

Understanding

Introduction. Jesus introduced his disciples to the God of their prayers by the term "Our Father," but he did not stop there. "Our Father, who art in heaven," he continued. Jesus seems here to be balancing the familiarity of the term Father with the awesome reverence implied in the phrase "who art in heaven."

For, as George Buttrick says in his book *So We Believe, So We Pray*:

Holiness . . . is implied in "which art in heaven." The exact translation is "which art in the heavens." . . . The very word heavens breathes holiness. Jewish reverence shrank from speaking the Divine Name; so holy is He that men must approach Him from afar, in such phrases as "which art in heaven." Thus the prayer "Our Father which art in heaven" invites the refining flame of Holiness.[1]

But beyond this view of holiness, what do we know of heaven and of the God who lives there?

Where and what is heaven? If we are honest about it, for most of us there is a great deal of confusion about the concept of heaven. Is it a place? or a time? Who lives there besides God?

The scriptures consistently refer to heaven as the dwelling place of God. But the understanding of heaven appears to have changed with the passage of time during the biblical period as well as since. William Barclay says, "Primitive Jewish thought conceived of the sky as a vast solid dome, set like a roof upon a square flat earth; and . . . beyond the dome of the sky there is heaven."[2]

Concordances list a variety of Hebrew words used in the Old Testament which are translated as heaven. Many of these words are human attempts to describe the physical qualities of heaven based upon this simple, spatial view of the universe.

In Daniel 2, however, the writer repeatedly uses the term the "God of heaven" as he contrasts the widsom and power of Daniel's God with the limitations of the gods of the Babylonians. The God of heaven is a God who "changes times and seasons . . . removes kings and sets up kings . . . reveals deep and mysterious things . . . knows what is in the darkness" (vv. 20–22) and "who reveals mysteries" (v. 28) and who makes known to people "the thoughts of [their] minds" (v. 30). The God of heaven also controls the movement of history (vv. 34, 35, 45) and will establish his own rule wordwide (vv. 35b and 44). The dwelling place of such a God must be a universal place of power and wisdom, no longer confined to a single spot in time and place.

New Testament writers built upon this image of heaven as the dwelling place of the all-wise and all-powerful God with the added dimension that it was also the dwelling place of the righteous dead. The Revelation to John is filled with images of such a heaven as well as commentary regarding future events on the earth. Chapter 4 describes one of John's visions of heaven. He describes an "open door" (v. 1), "a throne . . . with one seated on the throne" (v. 2) which he describes only in terms of the light, color, and brilliance of precious stones. We are told of "twenty-four elders" (v. 4) and of "four living creatures" (vv. 6–7) and of their continuous songs of praise (vv. 8 and 11).

John's description of heaven is poetic, and it speaks to our imaginations and feelings more than it informs our intellects. But his vision of heaven is one of continuous praise by the universal church (24 elders) and all of the elements of nature (the four beasts) of a God too great to be described in any human terms except symbols of dazzling beauty.

Heaven and the here and now. A story is told of a certain woman who in her earthly life enjoyed the lifestyle of wealth. She died and went to heaven. At the gate St. Peter called one of his angel helpers and said, "Please show this woman to her heavenly home."

The angel guide directed her through streets of large and extravagant mansions, and she could hardly contain her excitement, waiting to see which one was hers. The angel guide continued, however, farther out to the edge of the city where the houses became smaller and more modest. The woman was confused but she continued following her angel guide as she eyed the bungalows with disappointment.

Still the guide did not stop but continued even farther out of the heavenly city to an area of celestial slums where the dwellings could scarcely be called houses at all, so ramshackle were they. The angel guide stopped at the front door of one of the tiniest and said, "Here you are, ma'am. Welcome to your heavenly home."

"But," she protested, "this is barely a home at all. It is nothing but a shack. I can't possibly live in such a place for one day—let alone for all eternity."

"I'm sorry, ma'am," the angel guide replied, "but it was the best we could do with the building materials you sent ahead."

Jesus taught in many ways that heaven is related to the here and now. From John the Baptist (Matt. 3:2) he took up the message, "Repent for the Kingdom of heaven is at hand" (Matt. 4:17), and he sent that same message out with the disciples (Matt. 10:7). For Jesus, heaven was not just a place *out there* where God lived; it was also a condition of God dwelling in the heart of the believer. Heaven was now as well as not yet.

Jesus does not mention the word heaven in his parable of Lazarus and the rich man (Luke 16:19-31) and his account of the Last Judgment (Matt. 25:31-46). But in both it is clear that he is talking about the life after death and the eternal life of the righteous with God. His teaching in both stories is that the condition of life after death (heaven or hell) is a continuation of decisions made and actions taken during earthly life.

Lazarus and the rich man, the righteous and the unrighteous, are all surprised at what occurs in the afterlife, perhaps because their only view of heaven was of faraway majesty. Heaven is that. But, as the dwelling place of God, it is also in the heart of the believer who reverently prays, "Our Father, who art in heaven."

Discussion and Action

1. Share with the group the drawings or word pictures of heaven created by group members.

2. Finish this sentence: "Heaven is _____." Write the group's responses on a blackboard or newsprint.

3. How might your view of heaven differ from that of a refugee, a person who is hungry, or a political prisoner whose life is in danger?

4. What difference does it make to our lives—and to our prayer lives—that Jesus included the phrase "who art in heaven" in the model prayer he taught us?

5. Is heaven a place or a condition? Is it now or not yet?

6. Write down what you learned this week that was new about the Lord's Prayer.

1. George Buttrick, *So We Believe, So We Pray* (Nashville: Abingdon-Cokebury Press, 1951), pp. 136-37.

2. William Barclay, *The Daily Study Bible Series: The Revelation of John*, Vol. 1 (Philadelphia: Westminster Press, 1976).

4

Hallowed Be Thy Name
Exodus 3:1-15; Deuteronomy 18:9-22
Philippians 2:5-11

Preparation

1. Read the Lord's Prayer from various translations and paraphrases of the Bible, including *The Cottonpatch Version* by Clarence Jordan. Jot down different words used in translating the phrase "hallowed be thy name."

2. Look up the meaning of your name, both your family name and your given name. Does it describe you accurately? Who gave it to you?

3. As you read newspapers or listen to news broadcasts this week, evaluate which news stories hallow God's name and which do the opposite—desecrate or profane God's name.

Understanding

Introduction. In the third commandment, Exodus 20:7, the Lord says to his people, "You shall not take the name of the Lord your God in vain; for the Lord will not hold him guiltless who takes his name in vain." Jesus, in his model prayer, reinforces this reverence by stating it in a positive form, "Hallowed be thy name." But what does that mean, and how do we do it?

What's in a name? To the biblical writers, the name was far more than an identification tag. It represented the character and personal qualities of the person who bore it. See, for example, the stories of the naming of Jacob's twelve sons recorded in Genesis 29:31—30:24 and 35:16-20 and the story of Jacob wrestling with God (Gen. 32:24-30) in which he receives a new name when a change in character occurs.

God's name not only reveals God's nature but also serves as a connecting link between the high and holy God and the sinful humankind with whom God's saving presence also abides. God's name represents divine self-disclosure to human understanding.

In Exodus 3:1-15 we find the first biblical account of the revelation of God's name to a human. God has called Moses to go to Egypt and bring the people of Israel out of their bondage there. Moses voices to God a number of reasons why he thinks he is not the man for the job. One of those objections is that the Israelites will not know who it was that sent Moses to be their leader. Living in a society which worshiped a variety of gods, they would need more specific identification of this "God of your fathers." So Moses asks, "What is his name?"

God replies, "I AM WHO I AM," or, as the Hebrew words used imply both past, present, and future tense, it is sometimes translated as "I WILL BE AS I WILL BE" or "I CAUSE TO BE." In this name, God reveals a self that is creative, independent of other powers, the ground of being, and the essence of action and free will in relation to people. But, by revealing the name to Moses and his people, God also expresses a desire for communication and relationship with people.

But such a relationship will have special qualities which will honor the power of such a holy God. God's people are to live differently than their pagan neighbors who do not know God's name. In Deuteronomy are recorded many of the rules given by God through Moses to the Israelites to regulate their special relationship with the great I AM.

Rules for evaluating prophetic messages are recorded in Deuteronomy 18:9-20. All prophets who speak "in the name of other gods" are disqualified, but even those who speak "in the name of the Lord" must be tested. The people are to wait and see if the words spoken by the prophet "come to pass or come true." If not, even though he spoke in the name of the Lord, that prophet is not a spokesman for the God of Israel.

The "name of the Lord" therefore represents not only God's character but also God's power. But some who would use God's name do not possess God's power. They do not "hallow" God's name but rather "take it in vain"!

Hallow—not hollow. Clarence Jordan says in his book *Sermon on the Mount*:

> [Jesus] knew the awful tendency of the human heart toward hypocrisy. He knew that men could call God "Father," proclaiming themselves as his sons, and take the Father's name [as being in his family] and then keep right on living as sons of the Devil. They take God's name, but they take it in vain. They are play actors, hypocrites, using the Father's holy

name as a mask to cover their shameful iniquity. Jesus wanted no such people among his followers. Citizens of his kingdom—*Christ-ians*—were given a new name, and he intended that they should take it seriously and sincerely, and keep it ever sacred and holy.[1]

To "hallow" God's name is to fill it with reverence, worship, and obedience, not to use it empty and "hollow" for selfish or indulgent ends. The Old Testament prophet Amos thundered God's denunciation of Israel's empty religious rituals saying, "I hate, I despise your feasts, and I take no delight in your solemn assemblies . . . . But let justice roll down like waters, and righteousness like an ever-flowing stream" (5:21,24). The New Testament writer of the letter of James denounces the hypocrisy of showing favoritism to the rich in worship services (2:1-7).

Hallowing the name of God involves more than the proper word or the right ritual. It is a matter of obedience to Jesus Christ, as described in Philippians 2:5-11.

The self-humbling of Jesus Christ is portrayed in this early Christian hymn as an example for every believer. This humility is the means by which God offered salvation to us. It is also this great humility of Jesus the Christ that is the cause for God's "bestow[ing] on him the name which is above every name." The name is a name of power, a name due honor and reverence; it is Lord. Jesus is honored because he has hallowed God's name by humbling himself.

Julia Esquival, an exiled Guatemalan poet, reminds us in her book *Threatened with Resurrection (Amenazado de Resurrección)* that hallowing God's name is a current concern as well as a biblical one. In her poem "The Lord's Prayer from Guatemala" she writes:

Our Father, you who are here on earth . . . .

Your name is taken in vain,
    when they go around saying you are a little "anti-
        communist" god
who needs planes and tanks to crush the people
who are trying to forge their own history . . . .
And it is taken in vain,
    when they plan to smother our hunger for Justice
with presents from the surplus of the developed world.

Hallowed be your name,
in all those who defend the lives of the poor
above money, and coffee, and cotton, and sugar cane,
above political parties, and the laws
    and interests of Transnational Corporations.

Hallowed in the poor and humble
who still have faith and hope in you
and therefore organize themselves and struggle
so that their dignity be respected.

Hallowed in all those who work day and night
to free their brothers from illiteracy,
sickness, exploitation, and persecution.

Hallowed in the deaths of your saints . . .
and in the thousands of your children
who for the love of their brothers and sisters
and respect for the life of your poor,
were tortured and murdered
as was your Son,
Our Brother, Jesus Christ.[2]

Discussion and Action

1. Share with the group what you have learned about the meaning of your own name.

2. How do we hallow or desecrate God's name? With our words? With our lives?

3. Is profanity the only way we take God's name in vain? What about praying selfishly in Jesus' name?

4. How did you as an individual, or as a group, hallow God's name this week? When did you leave it hollow?

5. The coins of our nation's currency say "In God We Trust." Do we as a nation honor that statement? Is that hallowing or hypocrisy?

6. What did you learn this week that was new about the Lord's Prayer?

    1. Clarence Jordan, *Sermon on the Mount* (Valley Forge: Judson Press, 1952), p. 87.
    2. Julia Esquival, *Threatened with Resurrectión (Amenazado de Resurrección)* (Elgin, IL: Brethren Press, 1982), pp. 17-19.

5

Thy Kingdom Come,
Thy Will Be Done . . .
Matthew 22:1-14; Job 1; 2; 9; 42:1-6

Preparation

1. Read Luke's version of the wedding banquet (14:16-24); recall some of Jesus' other kingdom parables, such as those in Matthew 13; 18; 25; and Luke 12; 15.

2. Remember an occasion when you clearly discerned God's will for yourself.

Understanding

Introduction. We have come to the central focus of Jesus' model prayer for us: "Thy kingdom come, thy will be done on earth as it is in heaven." All the phrases that precede this and all the petitions that follow point to this central theme. When God's kingdom has come and God's will is fully done on earth, then God's name will be hallowed, all will have daily provisions, temptations will no longer beset us, and we will readily and completely forgive. But that glorious goal for which we pray—God's kingdom and will—is hazy to our earthly eyes. Where can we turn to get a clearer view?

The kingdom of God. Teachings and stories about the kingdom of God were the first and most frequent messages of Jesus. Clearly this theme was the central focus of his ministry. But when we examine his teachings we discover some confusing facts for he speaks of the kingdom in three different ways. He speaks of it in the past when he tells us that Abraham, Isaac, Jacob, and all the prophets were in the kingdom (Luke 13:28, Matt. 8:11). He speaks of it in the present when he says "The kingdom of God is within you (or among you)" (Luke 17:21). And he speaks of it in the future for he teaches us to pray for its coming and began some of his kingdom parables with, "When the Son of Man comes . . . " (Matt. 25:31) or "The kingdom shall be . . . " (Matt. 25:1).

One of Jesus' future images of the kingdom of God was a marriage feast. In the parable recorded in Matthew 22:1-14 he describes it and gives some additional insights into the nature of the kingdom. The guests were invited, not forced to attend, and when the invited guests refused, the banquet hall was filled with others, "both good and bad" (v. 10). Despite this "open admissions policy" the standards of righteousness are rigidly enforced upon those who enter there.

So the questions remain: How can the kingdom of God be both past, present, and future—both accepting and demanding?

Obviously that kingdom—that realm over which God is king—extends beyond the limits of our human understanding of time, space, and rules of behavior. It includes all those of every time, place, and lifestyle who love and obey its king. God's kingdom is—and has been throughout history—in the heart of every believer who elects God king of life. And it is our choice.

The will of God. This phrase does not appear in Luke's version of the Lord's Prayer. It, too, can be a confusing phrase. We pray for its coming and long for the day when it will be done perfectly, and yet we often associate it with suffering and tragedy. How can it be both desirable and distressing?

The story of Job wrestling with similar questions about the will of God is recorded for us by ancient biblical writers and poets. In chapters 1 and 2 we read of Job, a wealthy, righteous man who lost everything, including his health, because of the action of Satan which God permitted. Friends come to comfort him. In chapter 9 we see him alternating between despair and anger, between faithfulness and fear, as he seeks to understand God's will for him in this suffering.

Finally, in chapter 42:1-6, after a personal revelation of God, Job repents of his arrogance in attempting to comprehend God's will. He has seen the incomprehensible power and might of God (chaps. 38—41) and, in faith and humility, he accepts God's greatness and care.

The book of Job speaks eloquently to the questions in human minds about the will of God. But the questions persist. At the height of World War II, Leslie D. Weatherhead felt compelled to preach a series of sermons on this topic to his City Temple congregation.

The phrase "the will of God" is used so loosely as to land us not only in a confusion of mind but in a torment of feeling.

When a dear one dies, we call it "the will of God," though the measures we used to prevent death could hardly be called fighting against the will of God, and if they had been successful we should have thanked God with deep feeling that in the recovery of that dear one his will had been done . . . .

My own thinking demands a division of the subject into three parts . . .
1. The intentional will of God.
2. The circumstantial will of God.
3. The ultimate will of God.

The trouble arises because we use the phrase "the will of God" to cover all three, without making any distinction betwen them. But when we look at the Cross of Christ, we can see, I think, the necessity of such a distinction . . . .

1. It was not the intentional will of God, surely, that Jesus should be crucified, but that he should be followed. If the nation had understood and received his message, repented of its sins, and realized his kingdom, the history of the world would have been very different. Those who say that the Crucifixion was the will of God should remember that it was the will of evil men.

2. But when Jesus was faced with circumstances brought about by evil and was thrust into the dilemma of running away or of being crucified, then *in those circumstances* the Cross was his Father's will. It was in this sense that Jesus said, "Not what I will, but what thou wilt."

3. The ultimate will of God means, in the case of the Cross, that the high goal of man's redemption . . . a goal which would have been reached by God's intentional plan had it not been frustrated—will still be reached through his circumstantial will. In a sentence, no evil is finally able to defeat God or to cause any "value" to be lost.[1]

And so as we pray for the coming of God's kingdom and the doing of God's will on earth, we need also to pray for ourselves:

Lord, I know not what I ought to ask of thee; thou only knowest what I need . . . . I simply present myself before thee, I open my heart to thee. Behold my needs which I know not myself. Smite, or heal; depress me, or raise me up; I adore all thy purposes without knowing them; I am silent; . . . I yield myself to thee; I would have no other desire than to accomplish thy Will. Teach me to pray. Pray thyself in me. Amen.[2]

Discussion and Action

1. Which is your favorite of Jesus' kingdom parables? Why? Share with the group.

2. How can we know God's will for ourselves? Can we know it for someone else?

3. Do you agree with Leslie Weatherhead's division of the will of God into three parts? Does that make the concept clearer for you?

4. From what you know of the circumstances, would you consider this decade's famine and drought in Ethiopia to be God's intentional will, circumstantial will, ultimate will, or not the will of God at all?

5. What was your new learning about the Lord's Prayer this week?

1. Leslie D. Weatherhead, *The Will of God* (Nashville: Abingdon Press, 1944), pp. 22, 12, 23.

2. Reuben P. Job and Norman Shawchuck, *A Guide to Prayer for Ministers and Other Servants* (Nashville: The Upper Room, 1983), p. 39.

6

. . . Our Daily Bread
Exodus 16; Mark 8:1-21

Preparation

1. Write down on paper a list of your wants and another list of your needs. Are they the same?

2. Skip a meal this week and experience—in a temporary way—what hunger feels like.

Understanding

Introduction. In his lesson on prayer, Jesus moves abruptly from the spiritual to the physical: "Give us this day our daily bread." Both the adoration of God and the recognition of human needs are proper concerns for prayer, and our lives suffer when either is neglected.

Bread. All God's creatures need food; the Creator made us that way. In Jesus Christ, God experienced personally how human hunger feels. One of Jesus' wilderness temptations was to turn stones into bread (Matt. 4:3).

Almighty God knows also that his creatures need to trust their Creator for the needs of their lives. We are created that way but struggle with the human tendency to want to "do it ourselves." This age-old problem is reflected in many biblical stories where bread (food) is used as a symbol of the people's faith and trust in God.

For example, the Israelites, experiencing hunger and fear in the desert, decide that they prefer the food of Egypt to the freedom of the exodus. They begin to "murmur" against Moses and God. God provides them with food (manna) but sets limits upon its gathering which test their trust and obedience (Exod. 16: 4).

In Mark 8:1-10 is recorded the story of Jesus feeding the four thousand with seven loaves and a few small fish. The Bread of Life

(John 6:35), in faith and with thanks to God, transcended logic to meet the hunger needs of those who followed after him. But some still did not believe.

And we in today's world, like the Israelites in the desert and the hungry four thousand, need bread. And God continues to supply it—but unequally. The average calorie consumption per day in the United States is twice that in Haiti, Indonesia, India, and Iraq.[1] And hunger takes its toll; life expectancy in the United States (74.5 years in 1983) is 30 years longer than in Chad (43 years in 1981) and Haiti (45 years in 1984) and over two decades longer than in India (51 years in 1981).[2]

While Americans fight obesity, millions of persons in today's world lack food. They exist in a state of life-blighting hunger which we find difficult to envision:

> It seems that the slaughterhouse threw kerosene on their garbage dump so the *favelado* (slum dweller) would not look for meat to eat. I didn't have any breakfast and walked around half dizzy. The daze of hunger is worse than that of alcohol. The daze of alcohol makes us sing, but the one of hunger makes us shake. I know how horrible it is to only have air in the stomach . . . .
>
> The children eat a lot of bread. They like soft bread but when they don't have it, they eat hard bread.
>
> Hard is the bread that we eat. Hard is the bed on which we sleep. Hard is the life of the *favelado*.
>
> Oh, Sao Paulo! A queen that vainly shows her skyscrapers that are her crown of gold. All dressed up in velvet and silk but with cheap stockings underneath—the *favela* (slums).
>
> The money didn't stretch far enough to buy meat, so I cooked macaroni with a carrot. I didn't have any grease, it was horrible. Vera was the only one who complained yet asked for more.
>
> "Mama, sell me to Dona Julita, because she has delicious food."[3]

Why daily? God gives food to feed our bodies but sets limits upon that provision in order to feed our trust. Things have a way of insulating us against our dependence upon God's care. We trust in the freezer, the fast food restaurant, and the supermarket, rather than the God who supplies them all.

Except for on the Sabbath, the Israelites in the desert (Exod. 16) were permitted to gather only a single day's supply of manna. They were to trust God for tomorrow's food. That was asking too much of some and they tried to store a supply of manna overnight. It went to the worms!

Jesus warned the disciples against the "leaven of the Pharisees" (Mark 8:11-21). When they worried about their next meal, Jesus cautioned them against the influence of those who were tied to the tangible, always asking for a sign. They had just witnessed a miraculous feeding of four thousand people, but their faith in God was blotted out by attitudes that demand proof.

But are we, twentieth-century American Christians, immune from the leaven of the Pharisees? We, too, seek signs. Fostered by the electronic church, we seek the sign of an affluent lifestyle as proof of God's special blessing of us. But,

> I suggest that we are thieves in a way. If I take anything that I do not need for my own immediate use, and keep it, I thieve it from somebody else . . . . In India we have got three millions of people having to be satisfied with one meal a day, and that meal consisting of unleavened bread *(chapati)* containing no fat in it, and a pinch of salt. You and I have no right to anything that we really have until these three millions are clothed and fed better. You and I, who ought to know better, must adjust our wants, and even undergo voluntary starvation in order that they may be nursed, fed, and clothed.[4]

But change is possible, says Doris Longacre in her practical faith statement *The More-with-Less Cookbook*, and change is an act of faith.

> There is a way, I discovered, of wasting less, eating less, and spending less which gives not less, but more . . . .

> How can we continue overeating in the face of starvation, and be at peace with ourselves and our neighbors? "The destitute suffer physically, the overindulged morally," writes one Mennonite Central Committee relief administrator. When we begin eating less, the job is not finished. It is only beginning. If we expect North American food conservation to totally solve world hunger, with good reason we sound naive and even paternalistic. Concerned Christians will move on to initiate food production and distribution programs. They will challenge oppressive government policy.[5]

Again, as Jesus teaches us to pray for our daily bread, we need also pray for ourselves:

O God,
We've wasted, we've complained, we've grumbled.
We've misused our resources,
We've confused our needs with our wants.
For these sins, Father, forgive us.
Help us reset our priorities according to Your will. Amen.[6]

Discussion and Action

1. Share with each other how it felt to be hungry when you skipped a meal this week. Did this help you understand and feel compassion for the hungry of the world?

2. Have you ever lacked for daily bread and had to trust God for it? When? Share with the group.

3. What is the responsiblity of those with bread to those without?

4. List denominational programs or other agencies the group members are aware of that are combating hunger in your community and in other parts of the world. Some examples are Bread for the World, Heifer Project, and Global Food Crisis. Describe their ministries.

5. During the next four weeks plan, organize, and carry out a specific group response to hunger either in your own community or elsewhere in the world.

6. In reading the Lord's Prayer, I never realized before that
_____.

1. John Eagleson and Philip Scharper, *The Radical Bible* (Maryknoll, NY: Orbis Books, 1972).

2. *The World Almanac and Book of Facts* (New York: Newspaper Enterprise Association, Inc., 1986), pp. 783, 547, 566, 568.

3. "Child of the Dark: the Diary of Carolina Maria de Jesus" in *The Radical Bible* (Maryknoll, NY: Orbis Books, 1972), pp. 5-6, 85-86.

4. "All Men Are Brothers," *The Radical Bible* (Maryknoll, NY: Orbis Books, 1972), p. 13.

5. Doris Longacre, *The More-with-Less Cookbook,* (Scottdale, PA: Herald Press, 1976), pp. 12, 22-23.

6. *Ibid.*

7

Forgive Us . . . As We Forgive . . .
Exodus 21:1-11; Matthew 18:21-35 *Read 1.*

Preparation

1. Remember a time of giving and/or receiving forgiveness. How did it make you feel? Think of a time you refused to forgive or accept forgiveness. How did *that* make you feel? *2.*

2. Look up a dictionary definition of *forgiveness.* *3.*

Understanding

Introduction. Some of us say "debts," other Christians say "trespasses," depending upon which translation of the Bible has instructed us. But the meaning remains the same: "Forgive us our sins as we forgive the sins of others against us."

Jesus assumed this model prayer would be prayed by sinners, persons whose sins separated them from God and whose lack of forgiveness separated them from other people. So he moved directly from the petition for bread to nourish the body to this request for forgiveness to nourish the soul.

"Forgive us . . . " "For . . . all have sinned and fall short of the glory of God," Paul says in Romans 3:23, and John writes in his first letter, "If we say we have no sin, we deceive ourselves and the truth is not in us" (1:8). The more clearly we see the holiness of God, the more clearly will we see our sin. *≤ 4,*

> Sin is disobedience, straying from the will of God (Psa. 32:1); it is trespass . . . an informed and deliberate violation of the law (Isa. 53:8); it is . . . petulant rebelliousness of the human spirit . . . the pathetic emptiness of the creature trying to wage war with his Creator (Psa. 90:8); it is bondage . . . (Hos. 5:4).
>
> As a consequence of sin man has lost fellowship with God . . . [and] lives under God's wrath, filled with anxieties

and fears and out of harmony with nature and with his fellow men. Whereas God created him for a life of peace and harmony, he now lives in frustration. Forgiveness is the removal of the barriers between God and man.[1]

We sing and are debtors before God. We are also debtors to each other by acts of thoughtlessness and selfishness. In Old Testament times debt could result in slavery for the debtor (see Exod. 22:1 or 2 Kgs. 4:1). But God is more merciful than humans and their economic system, and in Exodus 21:1-11 we have recorded the laws given by this merciful One to provide "forgiveness" for debt slavery among the chosen people. After six years of service, Hebrew debt slaves could go free. The practice of freeing a debt slave after six years was the proclamation that God alone was the rightful owner of the Hebrew people, having redeemed them from slavery in Egypt (see Deut. 15:25). It prevented economic exploitation of the poor by the rich and "forgave" the debts of both slave and master by re-establishing equality in the economic order.

But we humans have rejected the mercy of God repeatedly over the centuries. Later writings of the Old Testament (for example, Amos 2:6) indicate that the Jews had great difficulty observing these laws promoting economic equality. And the sins of inequality in today's world of "haves" and "have-nots" continue to cry out for the forgiveness of similar debts of financial injustice.

The destruction of World War II left much of Europe in a shambles. The Marshall Plan offered financial assistance in both grants and loans for emergency relief and for the rebuilding of European industry. This aid was offered to former allies and former enemies alike and 16 European countries received over $13 billion of assistance from the United States. The motives for the plan were a mixture of forgiveness and economics, of kindness and politics. Stable European industry provided potential new trading partners for the US and undercut the influence being made by the Communist party in devastated Europe. Nevertheless, the Marshall Plan, in extending financial aid to former enemies, stands as an example of international forgiveness.

"As we forgive." Luke's version of the Lord's Prayer assumes human forgiveness has already taken place (see 11:4). But in Matthew's version, God's forgiveness of human beings is dependent upon their forgiveness of each other. As Clarence Jordan says: "One meets the Father on one's way *back* from being reconciled with his brother."

Our human failure to forgive each other was a problem which Jesus addressed repeatedly in the scriptures. Matthew 18 records a variety of these teachings. Verses 15-17 give a three-step procedure for seeking repentance and forgiveness of wrongdoing within the church family.

In verses 21-22, Peter questions, "How often must I forgive?" and Jesus' answer was to tell an unforgettable story (vv. 23-35). A servant owes the equivalent of $10 million to his king who kindly forgives him the entire amount. The servant, however, refuses to forgive $20 owed to him by a fellow servant and that refusal costs him his freedom when the king hears of his lack of mercy. The meaning of the parable is clear and unmistakeable, but Jesus must have known how often we are enslaved by unforgiveness. So he repeated his point at the end of the story (v. 35).

Why is forgiveness so difficult? What does it take to forgive? William Barclay says:

> We must learn to *understand*. There is always a reason why a person does something . . . . Forgiveness would be very much easier for us, if we tried to understand.
>
> We must learn to *forget*. So long as we remember and brood upon a slight or an injury, there is no hope that we will forgive . . . .
>
> We must learn to *love* . . . . Christian love, *agape*, is that . . . undefeatable good-will, which will never seek anything but the highest good of others, no matter what they do to us, and no matter how they treat us.[2]

In order to forgive, we must understand, forget, and love. But we must also remember—remember that God in Christ has forgiven us. Corrie ten Boom tells a story of such remembering in her book *The Hiding Place*.

For the "crime" of harboring Jews, she and her family were sent by the Nazis to concentration camps. She alone survived and returned to her native Holland. After the war she worked in ministry to those scarred by the war. Partly in order to raise money for this ministry, she did much public speaking, both in Holland and in Germany. Persons listened eagerly as she told of her experiences of God's presence with her in the concentration camp.

> It was at a church service in Munich that I saw him, the former S.S. man who had stood guard at the shower room door in the processing center at Ravensbruck. He was the first of our actual jailers that I had seen since that time. And suddenly it was all there—the roomful of mocking men, the heaps of clothing, [my sister's] pain-blanched face. He came up to me as the church was emptying, beaming and bowing.

"How grateful I am for your message, Fraulein," he said. "To think that, as you say, He has washed my sins away!"

His hand was thrust out to shake mine. And I, who had preached so often . . . the need to forgive, kept my hand at my side.

Even as the angry, vengeful thoughts boiled through me, I saw the sin of them. Jesus Christ had died for this man; was I going to ask for more? Lord Jesus, I prayed, forgive me and help me to forgive him.

I tried to smile, I struggled to raise my hand. I could not. I felt nothing, not the slightest spark of warmth or charity. And so again I breathed a silent prayer. Jesus, I cannot forgive him. Give me Your forgiveness.

As I took his hand the most incredible thing happened. From my shoulder along my arm and through my hand a current seemed to pass from me to him, while into my heart sprang a love for this stranger that almost overwhelmed me. And so I discovered that it is not on our forgiveness any more than on our goodness that the world's healing hinges, but on His.[3]

Discussion and Action

1. Why do we hold grudges? How does our lack of forgiveness enslave us and block God's forgiveness of us?

2. Brainstorm what God's new economic order might look like for our world of inequality. Record your ideas on newsprint.

3. Should the US institute an Asian equivalent of the Marshall Plan for the reconstruction of Vietnam? Why or why not? Does national pride affect forgiveness?

4. Close by praying together the Lord's Prayer. Picture in your mind any whom you have not forgiven. This week take some action to practice what we have just studied.

1. *The Interpreter's Dictionary of the Bible*, Vol. 2 (Nashville: Abingdon Press, 1962), p. 315.

2. William Barclay, *The Daily Study Bible Series: The Gospel of Matthew*, Vol. 1 (Philadelphia: Westminster Press, 1958), pp. 224-25.

3. Corie ten Boom, *The Hiding Place* (Washington Depot, CT: Chosen Books, 1971), p. 215.

8

Lead Us Not into Temptation . . .
Genesis 12; 22:1-18; Matthew 4:1-11

Preparation

1. Read Matthew 6:13 and Luke 11:4b in as many different translations as possible. Note the different terms used to translate
   this phrase. Check a Bible dictionary or commentary for its
   meaning.

2. Remember a time of temptation and testing in your personal
   life; in national life. What was the outcome?

Understanding

Introduction. Temptations surround us. In them we live,
move, and often feel we are drowning! But this petition from Jesus'
model prayer which should be so comforting raises many questions based upon the translation of the original Greek words. Bible
commentators translate it differently: "Do not bring us to hard testing" (TEV), "Do not let us be tested beyond our capacity to
endure" (Roger Shinn), or "And let us not succumb at the time of
trial" (Dr. Charles Cutler Torrey). One thing upon which most
translators agree is that to the biblical writers the word *temptation*
meant a testing or a trial to prove faith or obedience rather than
seduction or enticement to sin.

But this still raises questions. Should we pray to be spared
from testing if the purpose is to prove or strengthen our faith? Does
God lead us into temptation—or do we?

We lead us. Someone has said, "Everything I like to do is
either illegal, immoral, or fattening!" We cannot deny that much of
the temptation that besets us is of our own choosing. We are, in our
society, surrounded by situations which reward unfaithfulness to
God and by role models that subtly tempt us to adopt the ways of
the world.

But we cannot totally excuse ourselves on the basis of our corrupt contemporary society. Abraham dwelt in a much simpler culture but was tempted in a way which sounds amazingly modern. In a time of famine, Abraham was tempted to sacrifice the honor of his wife and God's promise of descendants in order to preserve his own life. He faces this temptation—and he falls! God preserves him in a miraculous way from the consequence of his unwise choices and faithlessness.

The New Testament story of Ananias and Sapphira (Acts 5:1-11) and Paul's touching comment in 2 Timothy that "Demas, in love with this present world, has deserted me . . . " (4:10) picture other generations which have, through unwise choices of their own, faced temptation and yielded to it.

Are we any different? The fast pace and complexity of our society changes the nature of the temptations we face, but it does not change the fact that we are faced with choices which test our faithfulness. And, like our spiritual ancestors, we sometimes fail the test.

The February, 1986, issue of the University of California's *Berkeley Wellness Letter* cites a major five-year study conducted at the Carter Center at Emory University in Atlanta, Georgia, which identifies "tobacco . . . as the single leading cause of death—1,000 deaths in America each day, all of them preventable . . . . Alcohol [was] the second most important risk factor."

We pray "lead us not into temptation" but continue to lead ourselves with unwise choices and lifestyles which undermine our faith in our Creator whose temple our bodies are! In such unwise choices it is not that God tests us but it is we who attempt to test God, the very height of unfaithfulness!

But perhaps Jesus understood our human tendency to blame God for the temptations and troubles which befall us—even those which we bring on ourselves! This petition which he taught us restores our faith in God as our protector, not our persecutor! So we pray, "Lead us not into temptation . . . " but our question remains, Does God ever lead us into temptation?

God leads us. The Bible records several instances in which wise and faithful choices led to testing or temptation. In Genesis 22:1-19 we read of a time when Abraham resisted the temptation to disobey and passed the test which God required of him. At God's request he obediently prepared to sacrifice his son Isaac, the child of his old age through which God's promise to him would be fulfilled. In earlier obedience, Abraham had sacrificed his past by leaving his homeland and family. Now God asks him to give up his future by sacrificing his son. Abraham clings to his faith that "God will provide" and, at the last moment, God does provide.

In Matthew 4:1-11 we read of Jesus' temptations in the wilderness. All three synoptic Gospels record that he was "led by the Spirit" and "tempted by the devil (or Satan)."

The temptation of Jesus is not an effort on the part of the devil to lure Jesus into committing some immoral act, but rather an attempt to force him to set aside his complete obedience to the will and purpose of God by adopting an easier means to the fulfillment of his mission. In the gospel tradition the devil . . . is waging an unsuccessful effort to wrest final control of the creation from God; i.e., the movement of history is the conflict between the kingdom of God and the kingdom of Satan. By offering him enticing possibilities, the devil is here pictured as trying to trick Jesus into submitting to his ways.[1]

Henry Nouwen writes in *Sojourners*:

Jesus . . . was tempted with the three compulsions of the world, to be relevant ("turn stones into loaves"), to be spectacular ("throw yourself down"), and to be powerful ("I will give you all these kingdoms") . . . . He affirmed God as the only source of his identity ("You must worship the Lord your God and serve him alone").[2]

God may lead us to where temptation exists but James reminds us that "God . . . himself tempts no one; but each person is tempted when he is lured and enticed by his own desire" (1:13-14). And Paul comforts us in 1 Corinthians with these words: "No temptation has overtaken you that is not common to man. God is faithful, and he will not let you be tempted beyond your strength, but with the temptation will also provide the way of escape, that you may be able to endure it" (10:13).

Drawing upon the wisdom of the desert fathers and mothers of the fourth and fifth centuries A.D., Henri Nouwen suggests three ways of escaping temptation:

Solitude is the furnace of transformation. Without solitude we remain victims of our society and continue to be entangled in the illusions of the false self. . . . [It] is the place of . . . the struggle against the compulsions of the false self and the encounter with the loving God who offers himself as the substance of the new self. . . . We enter into solitude first of all to meet our Lord and to be with him and him alone.[3]

Silence is the way to make solitude a reality. The Desert Fathers praise silence as the safest way to God. "I have often repented of having spoken," Arsenius said, "but never of having remained silent." . . . Christians have tried to practice silence as the way to self-control. It can be seen as a portable cell taken with us from the solitary place into the midst of our ministry. It is solitude practiced in action.[4]

Prayer. If solitude were primarily an escape from a busy job, and silence primarily an escape from a noisy milieu, they could easily become very self-centered forms of asceticism. But solitude and silence are for prayer . . . . The literal translation of the words "pray always" is "come to rest." . . . This rest, however, has little to do with the absence of conflict or pain. It is a rest in God in the midst of a very intense daily struggle. Abba Anthony even says to a fellow monk that it belongs to the great work of a man "to expect temptations to his last breath." . . . the rest which flows from unceasing prayer, needs to be sought at all costs, even when the flesh is itchy, the world alluring, and the demons noisy.[5]

Discussion and Action

1. What is temptation? Is it enticement to evil or testing of faith?

2. Is temptation always bad? Can any good result?

3. Does God lead us into temptation? Or do we lead ourselves? Why do we blame God?

4. What are some of your personal temptations? Share with the group how you deal with them. Do you find the spiritual disciplines of solitude, silence, and unceasing prayer helpful?

5. What did you learn new this week about the Lord's Prayer?

1. *The Interpreter's One-Volume Commentary on the Bible* (Nashville: Parthenon Press, 1971), pp. 613-14.

2. Henri Nouwen, "The Desert Counsel to Flee the World," *Sojourners,* June 1980, p. 16.

3. *Ibid.,* pp. 15-16.

4. Henri Nouwen, "Silence, the Portable Cell," *Sojourners,* July 1980, p. 22.

5. Henri Nouwen, "Descend with the Mind into the Heart," *Sojourners,* August 1980, p. 20.

9

... *Deliver Us from Evil*
2 Samuel 11; Matthew 27:45-54; Psalm 22

Preparation

1. Review some scriptures which deal with the evil one (Matt. 13:19; Eph. 6:16), the devil (Matt. 4:1; 1 Pet. 5:8), or Satan (Job 1; Luke 22:3; 2 Cor. 2:11).

2. Reflect on current news stories which tell of evil inherent in the structures of society. How do such evils affect the lives of persons?

Understanding

Introduction. EVIL—the very word causes our spines to tingle and creates mental images of bright red-horned beings carrying pitchforks or of gangsters carrying machine guns hidden in violin cases! When we pray not to be led into temptation we sense — that we do, after all, have a choice in the matter. But when we continue by asking for deliverance from evil, we admit our helplessness to deal with strong forces, entrenched and active in our world, which oppose God and his will. We can feel almost overwhelmed by "principalities . . . powers . . . rulers of this present darkness . . . spiritual hosts of wickedness" (Eph. 6:12). As Henri Nouwen writes: "Our society is not a community radiant with the love of Christ, but a very dangerous network of domination and manipualtion in which we can easily get strangled and lose our soul.[1]

Evil. In New Testament times people firmly believed in the power of the evil one to oppose the realm of God and do great harm in the world. Some Bibles give "deliver us from the evil one" in a footnote on Matthew 6:13 as an alternate translation of the phrase.

The influence of the evil one extended beyond individual persons to the structures of society. In Luke 4:5-7 the devil shows

Jesus all the kingdoms of the world. In exchange for Jesus' worship he offers to give Jesus "all this authority and their glory; for it has been delivered to me and I give it to whom I will." Clearly it was the devil's impression that all the nations of the world belonged to him, and we see much in our day to indicate that he continues to hold earth in bondage.

The struggle between good and evil is a basic theme of the Bible. Some of its most tragic stories describe times when personal evil was magnified by the structures of society—when evil used, for selfish ends, institutions that had been established for the benefit of others.

In 2 Samuel 11, for example, we have the revelation of some very dirty linen in the closet of King David. His personal evil of lust became adultery. In his attempts to conceal this sin he compounded the wickedness by exercising his royal rights as commander-in-chief of Israel's armies to practice deception, apostasy, and finally murder. He uses the social, political, and military structures of his society to cover up his personal iniquity.

It was the religious and political structures of his day which crucified Jesus (Matt. 27:11–54). No single person was to blame, but mob rule burned out of control when ignited by personal greed, fueled by power-hunger, and fanned by fear. And the evil one, using humans and structures, crucified the Son of God.

But the stories of corporate evil do not end in the New Testament. As George Buttrick says:

> Our age has evidence enough: we have seen evil, organized in demonic empire, calling falsehood by names of truth, delighting in wanton chaos and nothingness, until the whole planet is now under threat of atomic desolation. This is "the evil" with which we take chances, as we spin pleasant theories about "the ascent of man."
>
> At the onset of this century we were quite sure that we had war chained like a circus bear. We could fill our house with furniture and gadgets, and live in peace, and perhaps even conquer death. Then suddenly the tame bear, another disguise of the devil, was upon us. Perversity outside us and within has cankered over twenty civilizations. It has turned our technology into destruction and made democracies more warlike than kingdoms . . . .
>
> There is deliverance, or Jesus would not have taught us to pray for it . . . but woe to the man who thinks he can work his own deliverance.[2]

Deliverance. The German philosopher Nietzche said, "He who has a *why* to live for can bear with almost any *how.*" Viktor Frankl discovered in Nazi concentration camps that finding some meaning in life enabled humans to survive such evil. There is deliverance—but not within ourselves.

In Psalm 22 the psalmist begins with a cry for deliverance from the terrors of mortal illness. In despair he describes his pains and torments, the evils that encompass him. Searching for comfort, he recalls the history of his people and his own personal history but his despair returns. Finally, in total helplessness, he throws himself completely upon the mercy of God and his lament turns to thanksgiving.

Jesus quoted from this psalm as he hung on the cross (Matt. 27:46), and the psalm describes in prophetic detail the events of the crucifixion. It is the great mystery of the gospel how God used that evil event to secure our deliverance from the powers of evil.

King Christian X was monarch of Denmark when the country was invaded by the Nazis in 1940. He became a symbol of nonviolent resistance to the evils of the Nazi regime and emerged from prison after the war a hero among his countrymen. He offered no military resistance to the invading troops but, after the occupation, persisted in following his custom of riding horseback through the streets of Copenhagen among his subjects to show that he had not abandoned his claim to national sovereignty.

After the German occupation of Denmark, one of the first edicts passed by the Nazi-controlled government was that all persons of Jewish ancestry must wear a yellow Star of David at all times. Such a technique carried out in other occupied countries had marked Jews for discrimination and later persecution. In Denmark, however, the morning the edict went into effect, every Danish citizen, from the king to the humblest peasant, appeared on the streets wearing a yellow Star of David!

The king's resistance provided inspiration to his subjects who refused to have anything to do with the occupying troops. It was rumored that Nazi soldiers begged to be assigned to combat rather than to Denmark for it was easier to face bombs and bullets than the silent ostracism of the Danes!

Deliverance from evil does not always mean removal from evil. Sometimes it means faithfulness in its midst.

But deliver us from evil one;
who lurks in the Toyota jeeps
seeking to eliminate our physical life;
or behind the telescopic sights

with which they identify us
when we demonstrate in the streets.
The evil one embodied in the spies
who penetrate our communities
and our churches
in order to sentence us later on . . . .
Deliver us from those civilian and
    uniformed evil ones,
and deliver us from the evil which
    travels with a diplomatic pouch,
and, Lord:

deliver us from evil
which from our very depths
tempts us to live our life
by keeping to ourselves,
when you are inviting us to give it to our
    friends.[3]

Discussion and Action

1. List and discuss the news stories of this week which report the effects of evil in social structures.

2. What organizations are you acquainted with that work to offer deliverance to those caught in social evil? List them in a second column.

3. Decide on an action that the group can take together or as individuals to speak out against structural evil in our society or the world. Be prepared to report next week.

4. Write a paraphrase of the Lord's Prayer in words that are meaningful to you. Include some of the new learnings you have recorded during this study.

1. Henri Nouwen, "The Desert Counsel to Flee the World," *Sojourners,* June 1980, pp. 15-16.
2. George Buttrick, *So We Believe, So We Pray* (Nashville: Abingdon-Cokesbury Press, 1951), pp. 214, 216, 219.
3. Julia Esquival, *Threatened with Resurrection (Amenazado de Resurrección)* (Elgin, IL: Brethren Press, 1982), pp. 27-29.

10

For Thine Is the Kingdom, the Power and the Glory...
Isaiah 9:6-7; Revelation 5:6-14

Preparation

1. Listen to the "Halleluia," "Worthy Is the Lamb," or the "Amen" choruses from George F. Handel's oratorio *The Messiah*.

2. Rewrite the phrase we are studying in this chapter in more contemporary language.

3. Review all the texts of this study for evidences of God's dominion over creation.

Understanding

Introduction. Like the shout of celebration at the final buzzer of a sporting event, this doxology of praise bursts upon our consciousness at the end of this model prayer. It almost certainly came, not from the lips of Jesus, but from the faith and worship of the early church. Luke's record of the Lord's Prayer does not include this phrase and the earliest manuscripts of Matthew's Gospel also omit it.

Many translations of the Bible list this doxology only in a footnote, and for centuries prior to Vatican II the Roman Catholic church did not routinely use it in their liturgy. Most Bible commentators agree that this ascription of praise was added to Jesus' prayer by the early church and was modeled upon David's prayer of dedication of the temple gifts recorded in 1 Chronicles 29:11-13. If it is not a quote from Jesus, does it have any validity for us in our worship? Why was it added by the early church?

God's promise. The early church faced many obstacles such as persecution by society, the inevitable controversy within, and the specter of the shameful death experienced by their Lord. But they had the scriptures which recorded the prophecies and promises of God.

Isaiah 9:6-7 was a familiar and comforting image of God's promised Messiah. A king, representing all the best qualities of Israel's heroes, would come with power to rule forever and establish a kingdom of justice, righteousness, and peace.

In Revelation 5:6-14 John recorded his vision of the heavenly worship of the Lamb, the Risen Christ by whose sacrificial death the will of God is accomplished. His description of the glory of that scene includes images beyond human comprehension and joyous doxologies of praise offered by hosts of angels and saints.

The church's praise. Such promises were the nourishment on which that persecuted early church flourished and grew. In this doxology added to Jesus' model prayer, they praised the giver of those promises.

"For thine is *the kingdom*." It is the Greek word *basileia* that is translated "kingdom" in this passage. As we saw in earlier lessons, kingdom means rule or reign, and the central focus of Jesus' teaching was the kingdom of God. That kingdom is personified in Jesus, and our response to him determines the status of our citizenship. The early church knew whose they were!

"For thine is . . . *the power*." The Greek word *dunamis* is used here. It can also be translated as might, strength, or force and is the root of the English words dynamite and dynamo. In the face of persecution, the early church in this doxology remembers that it is not powerless but sustained by the "power that is made perfect in weakness" (2 Cor. 12:9).

"For thine is . . . *the glory*." The Greek word *doxa* used here indicates that glory is the part of the Divine which humans can see on earth. The Hebrew word *kabod* (glory) used in the Old Testament (see 1 Chronicles 29:11-13) has the additional connotation of weight, substance, honor, or dignity. Jesus Christ, the giver of the model prayer, was the glory of God; he was God's visible likeness on earth, his substance and honor. Jesus' crucifixion and resurrection were the utter glory of God and this, too, the church wanted to celebrate!

Our participation. Created from the heart and circumstances of the early church, does this little prayerful postscript speak to us? We do not face the persecution of ostracism and torture for our faith, but we are beset by more subtle forms of persecution. We struggle to separate the demands of the kingdom of the USA from the definition of the kingdom of God, to resist the temptation to define power solely in terms of "horses under the hood" or megatons, and to turn a blind eye to the advertising and TV talk shows touting the glory of movie stars and superheroes.

We, too, need to affirm whose we are and participate in this doxology. This has been our goal in this study. The study of the scriptures and the support and sharing with a small group are two useful tools for reaching that goal. But as we review the Lord's Prayer and summarize our learning from it, three other disciplines of the spirit are obvious.

Praying. In a society as busily active as ours, where every waking moment is usually filled with duties or clamor, prayer is too often overlooked in our search for something we "can do." The scriptures—and the Lord's Prayer in particular—remind us that we are not called "to do" God's work but "to be" God's people. Prayer is the occasion in which God shows us who we are and in which we show ourselves and our world whose we are.

As we saw in our first chapter, prayer is our act of allegiance. Chapters two through five acquainted us with various aspects of prayer such as our relationship and image of God, God's holiness and habitation, the meaning of reverence, and the focus of true prayer.

Trusting. Our society revels in Horatio Alger stories and admires the "self-made man." We fondly recall our pioneer history of hardy, independent spirits and are bombarded by TV commercials that announce, "Mother, I'd rather do it myself!" But the Lord's Prayer points us away from independence and self-sufficiency toward interdependence and dependence upon God.

In chapters six through nine, we studied Jesus' instructions to trust God for bread, forgiveness, guidance, and deliverance. The petitions are easy to understand; they are profoundly difficult to practice. But it was Mark Twain who said, "It is not the parts of the Bible I don't understand that bother me. It is the parts that I do understand!"

Living as if it were true already. So we come again to the prayer's closing doxology of praise: "For thine *is* the kingdom, power, glory...." We participate in this prayer when we underline the *is* and conduct our lives as if it were already true! The early church did not affirm that "thine *shall be* the kingdom, power and glory..." but "thine *is*...."

Many of our Christian ancestors lived what they called a "two kingdom theology." That is, they recognized that they were citizens of an earthly state but, because they were also citizens of a heavenly kingdom, they were called to conduct their lives differently than the norm of the society around them. The virtues of honesty, simplicity, non-resistance, piety, and community life guided their behavior in the midst of their societies of duplicity, materialism, power politics, humanism, and independence. Earthly life was, for them, a dress rehearsal for the heavenly kingdom which was their goal. As their descendents we, too, are called to live human lives as heavenly citizens, for the kingdom, power, and glory are God's.

The story is told of an English customs official who, in an age when smuggling and bribery provided extra income for his colleagues, steadfastly refused to compromise his integrity. On one occasion when an export-import dealer offered him a sizeable sum to illegally allow his shipment entry into the country, he again refused. The dealer, not able to comprehend the official's motivation for such self-sacrificing honesty, struck the table with his fist in exasperation and shouted profanely, "Why, for Christ's sake?" The customs official looked him directly in the eye and responded quietly, "Yes, that's it. For Christ's sake I cannot."

It was Jesus the Christ who taught his disciples—and us—to pray the Lord's Prayer. The simple phrases of that profound poem of faith teach us to pray, to trust, and to live as if it were true already—for Christ's sake!

Discussion and Action

1. How can we give evidence in our lives that we believe that the kingdom, the power, and the glory really are God's? Report on the actions you took as individuals or as a group this past week to speak out against evil in society.

2. What purpose is served by praise such as in this doxology and in those recorded in Revelation 5:9, 12-13?

3. Does this doxology have any meaning for us since it probably did not come from the lips of Jesus?

4. Review your "learning log" and share with the group some of the new insights you received about the Lord's Prayer during this study.

5. Celebrate your group and this time of study by holding hands around the circle and listening to the familiar musical setting of "The Lord's Prayer" by Malotte on record or cassette tape, or have a group member sing it. Then close by singing together the "Gloria Patri."